Spiders
and how they hunt

Jason Amber

Heinemann Educational Publishers
Halley Court, Jordan Hill, Oxford OX2 8EJ
a division of Reed Educational & Professional Publishing Limited

Heinemann is a registered trademark of Reed Educational & Professional
Publishing Limited

OXFORD MELBOURNE AUCKLAND
JOHANNESBURG BLANTYRE GABORONE
IBADAN PORTSMOUTH (NH) USA CHICAGO

First published 1999

07
10 9 8

British Library Cataloguing in Publication Data
A catalogue record for this book is available from the British Library.

ISBN 978 0 435 09685 4 *Spiders (and how they hunt)* single copy

ISBN 978 0 435 09686 1 *Spiders (and how they hunt)* 6 copy pack

Illustrations
All illustrations by Alan Male, Linden Artists.

Photos
Michael Leach / Oxford Scientific Films, page 6. J.A.L. Cooke / Oxford Scientific Films, page
7 top left and bottom left and page 24. Martin Wendler / NHPA, page 7 top right. Pascal
Goetgheluck / Ardea London Ltd, page 7 bottom right and page 10. Hans Christoph
Kappel / BBC Natural History Unit, page 8. Bob Fredrick / Oxford Scientific Films, page 12.
David M. Dennis / Oxford Scientific Films, page 14. Stephen Dalton / NHPA, page 16.
Garden Matters, 18. Mantis Wildlife Films / Oxford Scientific Films, page 20. A.N.T. / NHPA,
page 22.

Designed by M2
Printed and bound in China by China Translation & Printing Services Ltd.

Contents

Key

The symbols below are used in this book to show the habitats of the different spiders.

Desert   Grasslands   Woodland   Gardens   Ponds and lakes

Introduction

There are over 30,000 different species of spider, and they can be found all over the world. They are able to survive in hot and cold climates, in deserts, rainforests and grasslands. One can even live underwater. The only areas in which spiders are not found are the Arctic, the Antarctic and in deep oceans. All spiders are carnivores, but different species have different methods of catching their prey.

Arachnids

It is often thought that spiders are insects, but they are in fact a different kind of animal called an arachnid. There are significant differences between the two. Insects have six legs, whereas arachnids have eight. Typical insects are ants, bees, beetles and butterflies. Typical arachnids include spiders, scorpions and ticks.

	Insects	Arachnids
Legs	6	8
Antennae	2	none
Wings	most have 2 or 4	none
Has a poisonous bite or sting	some	nearly all
Eats plants	some	none
Eats other animals	some	all

Features of spiders

All spiders:
- have eight legs;
- have large jaws and sharp fangs to bite prey;
- have spinnerets that can spin silk for making webs.

Most spiders:
- have eight eyes, but many cannot see very well;
- have hairs on their legs that can sense the movement of other animals nearby;
- have fangs through which they can inject poison into their prey.

Some spiders:
- have six, four or two eyes;
- have no eyes at all — these are cave-dwelling spiders.

claw

eyes

fangs

hairs

jaw

head and thorax

abdomen

spinnerets

leg

Spiders, like all arachnids, are divided into two body parts: the head and thorax, and the abdomen.

5

Catching prey

All spiders eat other animals. They bite their prey, then most inject a poison that kills or paralyses their victim, making them ready to eat. Different spiders catch their prey in different ways: some ambush their prey, lying in wait until their prey comes near enough to attack; some are hunters, and move around looking for prey; others use silk to help them trap their prey.

Don't kill spiders!

Some people are afraid of spiders and even kill them. Only a few kinds of spiders, all of which live in hot countries, are dangerous to people, and they will only bite if they are attacked. Most spiders cannot, or do not, bite people and are harmless. Spiders are also very useful because they kill insects, such as flies and cockroaches, which spread diseases.

Many spiders build webs of silk to catch their prey.

Eyes, jaws and legs

Spiders that run around hunting their prey need to have good eyesight, so they usually have large eyes.

Spiders that lie in wait to ambush their prey, or that catch their prey on webs, do not need to see for long distances, therefore they usually have small, weak eyes.

Jumping spider

Orb web spider

Crab spider

Spiders that catch their prey by grabbing them before they bite them generally have strong legs.

Purse web spider

Spiders that catch their prey by impaling them on their jaws usually have huge stabbing fangs.

Habitat	Size	Latin family name
	13–40mm	Ctenizidae

Ambush spiders

Trapdoor spiders

These large spiders make burrows in the ground using their powerful jaws like pickaxes to dig the soil. They line their burrow with silk and make a door from a mixture of soil and silk. They hide in their burrow, safe from enemies, waiting for their prey.

• Trapdoor spiders usually ambush passing insects at night.

8

Prey capture

1 The trapdoor spider lies in wait just behind the burrow door, waiting for a small creature to walk past. Some trapdoor spiders also spin lines of silk around their door that act like trip wires.

2 The spider keeps its legs touching the trip wires. When a passing insect touches a trip wire the spider opens its trapdoor and rushes out. It bites the insect with its huge jaws, injecting it with poison.

3 In a flash, the spider pulls the insect back into its burrow to eat.

9

Habitat	Size	Latin family name
	12–17mm	Atypidae

Ambush spiders

Purse web spiders

Purse web spiders dig burrows similar to those dug by trapdoor spiders (see page 8). They weave a tube of silk that comes out of the burrow and lies across the ground. The tube is camouflaged by a covering of soil. The purse web spider hides inside the tube, waiting for its prey.

Purse web spiders have huge fangs.

Prey capture

1 The purse web spider waits inside its tube. When an insect lands on the tube it cannot see the spider; however, the insect's movements make the tube vibrate, so the spider is aware of the insect's presence.

2 With incredible speed the spider runs underneath the insect and stabs its huge fangs through the silk and up into the victim's belly.

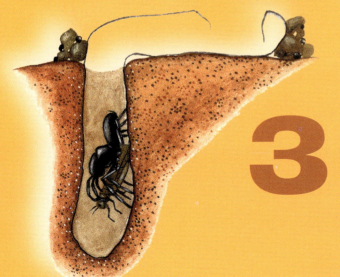

3 It then pulls the insect down inside the tube and drags it into its burrow to eat.

Habitat	Size	Latin family name
	4–15mm	Thomisidae

Ambush spiders

Crab spiders

These squat, round spiders have large front legs and resemble small crabs. They even walk sideways like a crab. They sit on flowers or under stones, waiting for their prey to come within range. They even attack large prey like bumblebees.

Crab spiders are camouflaged so they are hard to spot.

Prey capture

1 The crab spider waits on a flower head. It will stay there for the whole day, motionless, waiting for an insect to land on the flower.

2 When an insect lands on the flower, the crab spider remains motionless. Gradually it approaches the unsuspecting insect.

3 Anchoring itself to the flower with its strong back legs, the spider uses its large front legs to grab the insect. It bites the insect behind the head and injects it with poison. Then it slowly sucks out the insect's insides.

13

Habitat	Size	Latin family name
	4–34mm	Lycosidae

Hunters

Wolf spiders

These large spiders have long legs and large eyes. Their long legs help them to run fast, both on land and across water. Their large eyes give them sharp sight and all-round vision. Some wolf spiders live by ponds, running across the surface of the water to snatch up drowning insects.

Wolf spiders always hunt alone.

Prey capture

1 The wolf spider runs along the ground looking for prey.

2 When it sees an insect, the spider stands still. Then it creeps slowly towards its prey, like a cat stalking a mouse.

3 Suddenly, with a burst of speed, it charges at the insect and bites it. The poison soon paralyses the insect and the spider eats it.

Habitat	Size	Latin family name
	4–15mm	Salticidae

Hunters

Jumping spiders

These small spiders have short, strong legs and huge eyes. Their powerful legs enable them to jump great distances (up to 40 times their own body length). Some can even leap up into the air to catch flying insects. Jumping spiders' big eyes give them the best eyesight of all spiders.

The tiny hooks on a jumping spider's feet enable it to walk up walls and even up glass without falling off.

Prey capture

1 The jumping spider runs along the ground or up walls or trees looking for prey. When it sees its prey it stands still, then approaches very slowly so it is not seen.

2 Suddenly the spider jumps at the insect. It spins a 'life-line' of silk behind it, attached to the ground. If the spider misses and falls, it can pull itself back up its life-line.

3 The spider lands on its prey and injects it with poison.

Habitat	Size	Latin family name
	3–45mm	Araneidae

Orb web spiders

Orb web spiders spin large webs that act like fishing nets to catch flying insects in their sticky silk threads. The spider will eat anything that gets caught in its web, day or night. However, if a dangerous insect like a wasp gets caught in the web, the spider may cut the silk to release it rather than risk getting stung.

Orb web spiders spin webs that are very strong and yet almost invisible.

18

Prey capture

1 The orb web spider has very poor eyesight, so it uses the sensitive hairs on its legs and feet to detect approaching prey. It waits in the middle, or hub, of its web, or hides in a silk lair next to the web. It rests its feet on 'signal' threads leading from the web.

2 When an insect flies into the web it struggles, causing the web to vibrate. The spider feels these vibrations with its feet. It can tell from the vibrations exactly how big the trapped prey is and even if it is a dangerous insect like a wasp. The spider rushes out and bites its prey.

3 Once the prey has been paralysed, the spider wraps it in silk. It carries it to the middle of the web or back to its lair to eat.

19

Habitat	Size	Latin family name
	10–18mm	Dinopidae

Net throwers

Net throwing spiders are nocturnal. They do not sit in their webs like other spiders; instead they weave a small and elastic net of silk, which they hold in their front legs to catch their prey. They can drop this net onto passing insects or spread it in front of moths to catch them as they fly by.

A net throwing spider holding its net. At dawn it may hang the net up on a leaf, ready to collect again the following night.

Prey capture

1 The net throwing spider hangs head first, just above the ground, holding its web net in its front legs.

2 When an insect passes, the spider stretches its net out so it becomes much bigger. It holds its net above the insect.

3 The spider pushes the sticky net down over the insect, wraps the prey up in the web, and paralyses it with a bite.

21

Habitat	Size	Latin family name
	5–18mm	Mastophora

Bolas spiders

These small, fat spiders spend the day hiding beneath leaves. At night they come out and hang beneath a twig waiting for their prey. They catch them in an amazing way using a 'bolas'. This is a thread of silk with a large sticky droplet on the end.

This spider is swinging its bolas. · · · · · · · ·

Prey capture

1 The bolas spider hangs from a line of silk. It spins another thread of silk with a sticky droplet on the end, and lets this 'bolas' hang down like a fishing line.

2 When a moth flies near, the spider begins to swing the bolas.

3 As the moth gets closer, the spider suddenly swings the bolas out at it. The moth gets stuck on the sticky end of the thread. Slowly the spider pulls in the thread and bites the moth.

23

Habitat	Size	Latin family name
	15mm	Argyroneta

Water spiders

These small arachnids are the only spiders that live underwater. They make an amazing underwater home by weaving a web between weeds. Then they drag air bubbles under the water and push them into the web. The air bubbles get trapped in the web, allowing the spider to live and breathe in this dome-shaped bubble of air.

This water spider is filling its nest with air bubbles.

Prey capture

1 The water spider sits inside its nest, breathing the air, waiting for prey. It has very sensitive hairs on its legs that can detect even small movements in the water nearby.

2 The spider senses an insect crawling near the nest.

3 The spider rushes out and bites the prey, injecting it with poison, before carrying it back into the nest to eat.

Telling spiders apart

This Venn diagram will help you tell different spiders apart

FAST RUNNER

Wolf spider

Jumping spider

WAITS ON FLOWER FOR PREY

Crab spider

SPINS SILK TO CATCH PREY

Bolas spider

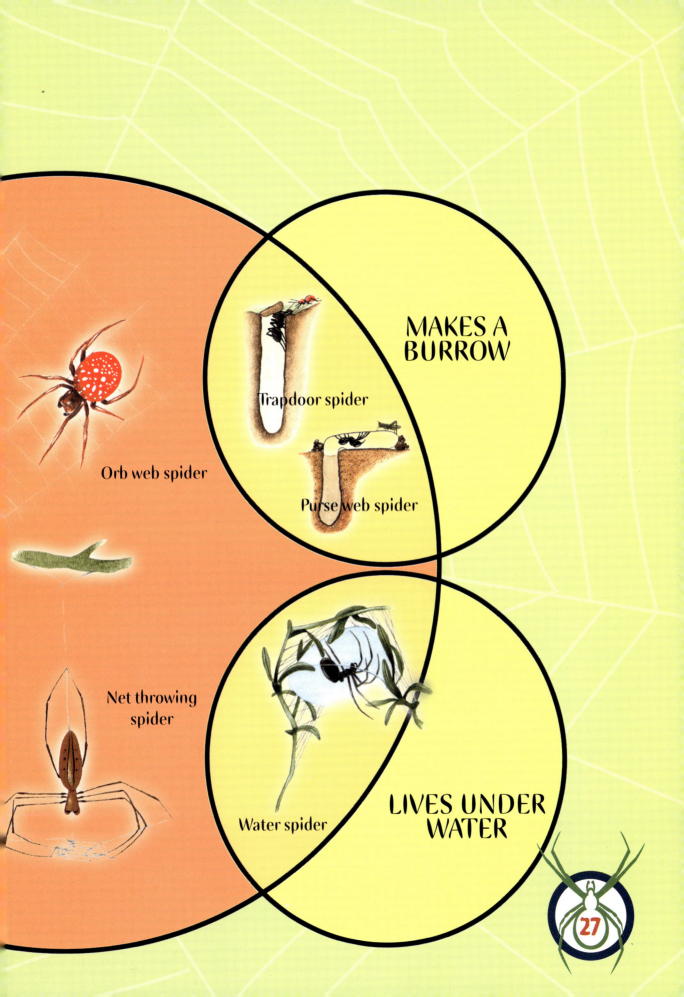

MAKES A
BURROW

Trapdoor spider

Purse web spider

Orb web spider

Net throwing
spider

Water spider

LIVES UNDER
WATER

Hunting flow chart

This flow chart describes the different ways spiders hunt.

Spins silk to catch prey

→ Makes a burrow →

→ Makes a web to live by or in →

→ Throws web or swings silk at prey →

Does not use silk to catch prey

→ Good eyesight →

→ Poor eyesight →

Makes a trapdoor at end of burrow	⮕	Trapdoor spider
Makes a silk tube at end of burrow	⮕	Purse web spider
Catches insects that live underwater	⮕	Water spider
Catches flying insects	⮕	Orb web spider
Catches prey with a small silk net	⮕	Net throwing spider
Catches prey with a single line of silk	⮕	Bolas spider
Fast runner	⮕	Wolf spider
Good at jumping	⮕	Jumping spider
Lives on flowers	⮕	Crab spider

Glossary

abdomen
the rear part of an arachnid or insect's body

antennae
two tubes on an insect's head, used to smell, feel or hear

carnivore
an animal that eats other animals

impale
to stab

lair
burrow, nest or home

nocturnal
active during the night

paralysed
unable to move normally

prey
an animal that is hunted by another for food

silk
very thin but strong thread produced by spiders and some insects

species
a group of living things that are very similar

thorax
the middle part of an arachnid or insect's body

vibrate
to shake very quickly

Bibliography

Harlow, Rosie and Morgan, Gareth, *Minibeasts*,
Fun with Science, Kingfisher, 1991

Hillyard, Paul, *Spiders Photoguide*, Collins Gem,
HarperCollins Publishers, 1997

Kalman, Bobbie, *Web Weavers and Other Spiders*,
Crabtree Publishing Co, 1997

Parsons, Alexandra, *Amazing Spiders*,
Eyewitness Juniors, Dorling Kindersley, 1990

Preston-Mafham, Ken, *Spiders—The illustrated identifier to over 90 species*,
The Apple Press, 1998

Preston-Mafham, Rod and Ken, *Spiders of the world*,
Blandford Press, 1989

Preston-Mafham, Rod and Ken, *The Natural History of Spiders*,
Crowood Press, 1996

Preston-Mafham, Rod, *Spiders, an illustrated guide*,
Blandford Press, 1991

Theodorou, Rod and Telford, Carole, *Spider and Scorpion*,
Spot the Difference, Heinemann Library, 1997

Watts, Barrie, *Spider's Web*,
Stopwatch Books, A & C Black, 1990

Index